A Day in the Life: ... nals

Red Kangaroo

Anita Ganeri

Raintree is an imprint of Capstone Global Library Limited, a company incorporated in England and Wales having its registered office at 7 Pilgrim Street, London, EC4V 6LB – Registered company number: 6695582

First published in hardback in 2011
First published in paperback in 2012

Edited by Daniel Nunn, Rebecca Rissman, and Sian Smith
Designed by Richard Parker
Picture research by Elizabeth Alexander
Production by Victoria Fitzgerald
Originated by Capstone Global Library Ltd
Printed and bound in China by South China Printing Company Ltd

ISBN 978 1 406 21963 0 (hardback)
14 13 12 11 10
10 9 8 7 6 5 4 3 2 1

ISBN 978 1 406 22126 8 (paperback)
15 14 13 12
10 9 8 7 6 5 4 3 2 1

British Library Cataloguing in Publication Data
Ganeri, Anita, 1961-
Red kangaroo. -- (A day in the life. Desert animals)
1. Red kangaroo--Juvenile literature.
I. Title II. Series
599.2'223-dc22 .

Acknowledgements
We would like to thank the following for permission to reproduce photographs: Alamy pp. 11 (© Arco Images GmbH), 15 (© Juniors Bildarchiv), 19, 23 glossary mammal (© Avico Ltd), 20 (© David Hosking); Corbis pp. 5, 23 marsupial, 23 glossary pouch (© Frank Krahmer), 8 (© Martin Harvey), 13, 14, (© Frans Lanting); FLPA p. 21 (Tom and Pam Gardner); Photolibrary pp. 7, 23 glossary desert (Image Source), 9 (Corbis), 10, 22 (Konrad Wothe/ OSF), 12, 23 glossary graze (Jim Tuten/OSF), 16, 23 glossary mob (Gerard Lacz/Peter Arnold Images), 17, 23 glossary dingo, 23 glossary predator (Jurgen + Christine Sohns/Picture Press), 18 (Root Alan and Joan/OSF); Shutterstock p. 4 (© Rafael Ramirez Lee).

Front cover photograph of a red kangaroo (Macropus rufus) in Finke Gorge National Park, Australia, reproduced with permission of FLPA (© Frans Lanting).

Back cover photograph of (left) a kangaroo's pouch reproduced with permission of Corbis (© Frank Krahmer); and (right) a red kangaroo in the Australian Outback, reproduced with permission of Photolibrary (Corbis).

We would like to thank Michael Bright for his assistance in the preparation of this book.

Contents

Some words are shown in bold, **like this**.
You can find them in the glossary on page 23.

What is a red kangaroo?

A red kangaroo is a **mammal**.

All mammals have some hair on their bodies and feed their babies milk.

Red kangaroos belong to a group of mammals called **marsupials**.

A female marsupial has a **pouch** on her body where her baby feeds and grows.

Where do red kangaroos live?

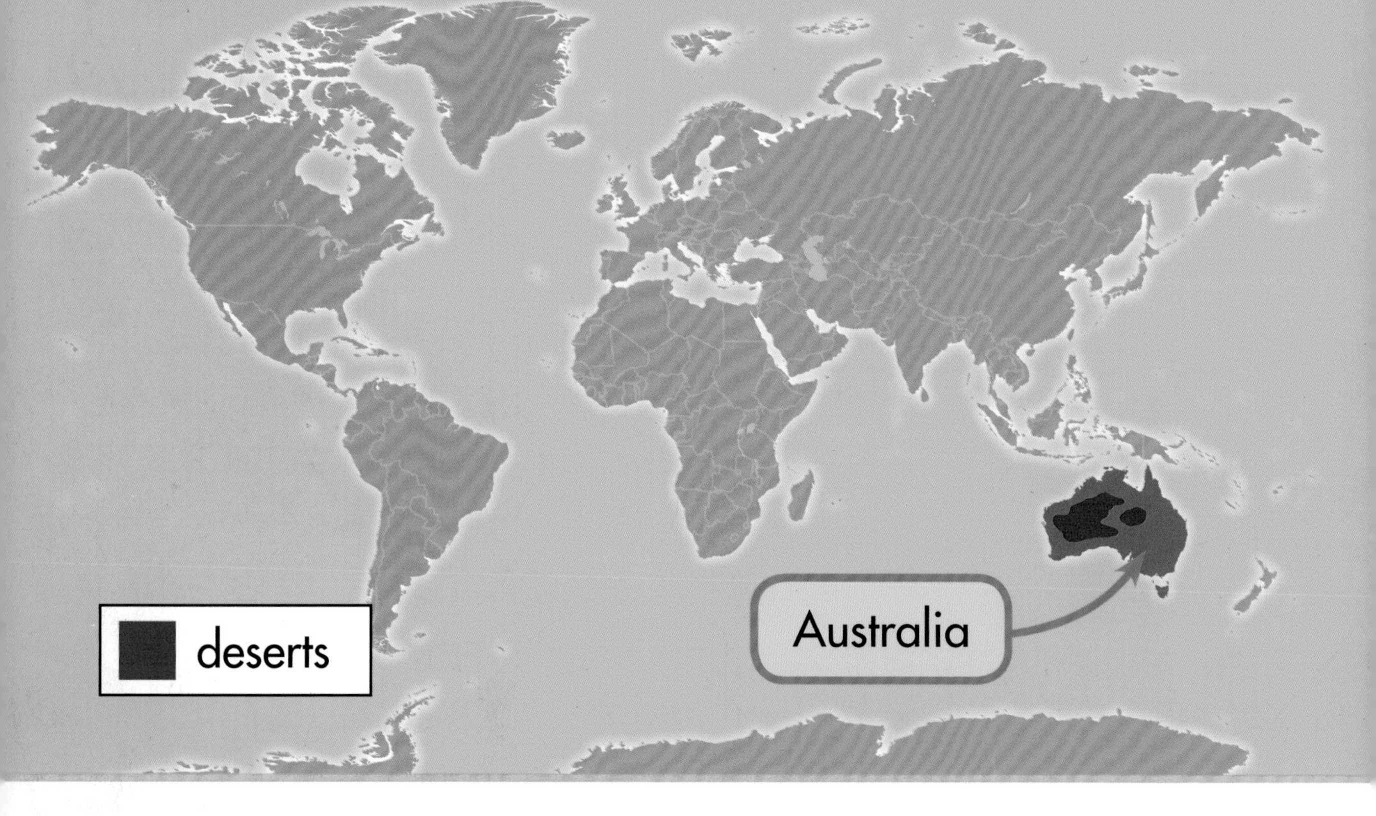

Red kangaroos live in the **deserts** of Australia.

Can you find these deserts on the map?

It is hot and dry in the desert.

The ground is mostly rocky and sandy, and there are only a few trees for shade.

What do red kangaroos look like?

Red kangaroos are big and strong, with short, red-brown fur.

Males are larger than females, and stand taller than an adult human.

Kangaroos have huge back legs and feet for hopping.

Their front legs are much shorter.

What do red kangaroos do in the evening?

In the day, it is very hot in the **desert**.

Red kangaroos start looking for food in the evening, when it is cooler.

A red kangaroo may **graze** all night long if there is plenty of food.

Its eyes are very good at seeing in the dark.

What do red kangaroos eat?

Red kangaroos **graze** on grass and other **desert** plants.

They sit on their back legs, and lean down to feed.

There is not much water in the desert, but red kangaroos can go for a long time without drinking.

They get water from the plants they eat.

How do red kangaroos move?

At night, red kangaroos travel long distances to find food.

They move by hopping on their huge back legs.

A red kangaroo hops along in giant leaps.

It uses its long tail to help it balance as it hops along.

Do red kangaroos live in groups?

Red kangaroos usually live in small groups of up to ten animals.

A group of kangaroos is called a **mob**.

While the kangaroos eat, they listen out for **dingos** and other **predators**.

The kangaroos thump the ground with their feet to warn the others of danger.

What do baby red kangaroos look like?

A new-born red kangaroo, or joey, is only about the size of a bee.

It crawls into its mother's **pouch** where it drinks milk and grows.

When the joey is about seven months old, it comes out of the pouch for the first time.

But it hops back in if it is frightened.

What do red kangaroos do in the day?

In the morning, red kangaroos stop **grazing**.

They find a shady tree where they can spend the day resting or sleeping.

If a red kangaroo gets too hot, it sometimes licks its front legs to cool down.

In the evening, it starts grazing again.

Red kangaroo body map

Glossary

desert very dry place that is rocky, stony, or sandy

dingo type of wild dog that lives in Australia

graze feed on grass and plants

mammal animal that feeds its babies milk. All mammals have some hair or fur on their bodies.

marsupial mammal with a pouch on its body

mob group of kangaroos

pouch like a big pocket

predator animal that hunts other animals for food

Find out more

Books

Desert Animals (Focus on Habitats), Stephen Savage (Wayland, 2006)

Deserts (My World of Geography), Angela Royston (Heinemann Library, 2004)

24 Hours: Desert (Focus on Habitats), Elizabeth Haldane (Dorling Kindersley, 2006)

Websites

Look at photos and videos of red kangaroos at:
www.arkive.org/red-kangaroo/macropus-rufus

Learn more about red kangaroos at:
www.sandiegozoo.org/animalbytes/t-kangaroo.html

Index